PARANORMAL LIFE CYCLES

GOBLIN

By
Noah Leatherland

©2024
BookLife Publishing Ltd.
King's Lynn, Norfolk
PE30 4LS, UK

All rights reserved.
Printed in India.

A catalogue record for this
book is available
from the British Library.

ISBN 978-1-80505-680-5

Written by
Noah Leatherland

Edited by
Robin Twiddy

Designed by
Drue Rintoul

All facts, statistics, web addresses and URLs in this book were verified as valid and accurate at time of writing.
No responsibility for any changes to external websites or references can be accepted by either the author or publisher.

AN INTRODUCTION TO BOOKLIFE RAPID READERS...

Packed full of gripping topics and twisted tales, BookLife Rapid Readers are perfect for older children looking to propel their reading up to top speed. With three levels based on our planet's fastest animals, children will be able to find the perfect point from which to accelerate their reading journey. From the spooky to the silly, these roaring reads will turn every child at every reading level into a prolific page-turner!

CHEETAH

The fastest animals on land, cheetahs will be taking their first strides as they race to top speed.

MARLIN

The fastest animals under water, marlins will be blasting through their journey.

FALCON

The fastest animals in the air, falcons will be flying at top speed as they tear through the skies.

IMAGE CREDITS

All images courtesy of Shutterstock.com. With thanks to Getty Images, Thinkstock Photo and iStockphoto. Cover – Luca Lorenzelli, Sergio Photone, Here, Jakub Krechowicz, sociologas, wabeno. Recurring – Elizaveta Mironets, sociologas, wabeno. P1 – Luca Lorenzelli. P4–5 – JGade, elebeZoom. P6–7 – tsuneomp, Joeprachatree. P8–9 – B-D-S Piotr Marcinski, nobeastsofierce, Gustavo Tabosa. P10–11 – xpixel, KYNA STUDIO, Katrina Bianchi. P12–13 – Holiday.Photo.Top, PixelSquid3d, tsuneomp, SmileStudio. P14–15 – Sporto8, NisanatStudio, Steve Collender, feltto. P16–17 – Sporto8, Matthew Troke. P18–19 – AKaiser, Wachiwit, ismail albayrak, DomCritelli, Holiday.Photo.Top. P20–21 – Philll, Garno Studio, tsuneomp, Oleksandr Khoma. P22–23 – Declan Hillman, DM7. P24–25 – Natalie Board, Pixel-Shot, xpixel. P26–27 – Benedek Alpar, RJ22, New Africa, Adam Radosavljevic, LightField Studios. P28–29 – antpkr, tsuneomp. P30 – OP38Studio.

CONTENTS

- **PAGE 4**   What Is a Life Cycle?
- **PAGE 6**   What Is a Goblin?
- **PAGE 8**   The Curse Begins
- **PAGE 10**   The Early Goblin
- **PAGE 12**   The Fully Transformed Goblin
- **PAGE 14**   Diet
- **PAGE 16**   Habitat
- **PAGE 18**   The Old Goblin
- **PAGE 20**   Passing on the Curse
- **PAGE 22**   Types of Goblin
- **PAGE 24**   Spotting a Goblin
- **PAGE 26**   How to Deal with a Goblin
- **PAGE 28**   Life Cycle of a Goblin
- **PAGE 30**   Beware the Paranormal!
- **PAGE 31**   Glossary
- **PAGE 32**   Index

Words that look like <u>this</u> can be found in the glossary on page **31**.

WHAT IS A LIFE CYCLE?

Every living thing has a life cycle. Over their life cycle, a living thing grows and changes.

Eventually, it will die. Living things <u>reproduce</u> so that the cycle can carry on after they are gone. This is all a normal part of the life cycle.

However, not everything in this world is normal. Some things just cannot be explained. Some things are paranormal.

There could be something paranormal living near you right now. Lots of people cross paths with paranormal creatures without even knowing it.

This is what happens in the gross life cycle of a goblin…

WHAT IS A GOBLIN?

Goblins are gross creatures that make a lot of mess wherever they go. Goblins have been found all over the world. Nowhere is safe from their mischief.

Goblins are <u>pests</u>. They find their way into places where they should not be and make a home there.

Be careful. Goblins can be very hard to find and very hard to get rid of. You do not want them anywhere near you.

Goblins have a very strange life cycle. They are not born. They do not hatch from eggs. Instead, they have a much nastier start to their lives.

THE CURSE BEGINS

The world is full of magic. Not all this magic is good. When an evil magic mixes with mud, it can create goblin spores.

Goblin spores are so small that humans cannot see them. The spores float in the air and make a horrid smell. When people breathe the spores in, they stick to the hairs inside their nose.

Spores

Inside a human's nose, the spores mix with the next part needed for the goblin's curse – snot. When someone sneezes, these snotty spores are sent out into the world.

The snotty spores eventually settle somewhere damp. It could be a muddy puddle, a wet spot near a toilet or even the gross spot next to a drainpipe.

THE EARLY GOBLIN

The first stage of the life cycle comes after the snotty spores have settled... and it is truly disgusting. Lumps of dark green goo spring up around where the spores landed. This is goblin gunk.

Goblin gunk is very sticky. As well as growing on the ground, goblin gunk can stick itself to walls and even ceilings.

Goblin gunk

Inside these blobs, some of the gunk starts to <u>transform</u>. It hardens and becomes the body of the goblin.

The piles of goblin gunk start to look like they are wobbling. They begin bubbling and boiling as the goblin grows inside. You might even start to hear the baby goblin squealing.

THE FULLY TRANSFORMED GOBLIN

After about an hour of gurgling inside the gunk, the next part of the goblin's life cycle takes place. Sharp claws stretch out of the ends of their thin fingers.

The new goblins use their claws to slice their way out of the gunk. Then they join up with the other goblins that came from piles of gunk nearby.

Fully transformed goblins are very small. Their green bodies are very skinny and bony. They are usually around ten centimetres tall.

They have pointy ears that can hear things that are too quiet for humans to hear. This means that goblins can talk to each other without humans hearing them.

DIET

Although they are only small, goblins have very hard teeth. Their teeth are able to chomp nearly anything into tiny pieces.

Because of their size, there are not many creatures that they can hunt. So, goblins eat whatever they can get their hands on. Usually, this is whatever is left on the floor.

Old toenails, lost coins and forgotten hair ties are all big parts of a goblin's diet.

Socks are their favourite tasty treats. Most of the time, they only manage to drag one sock out of the drawer. So, if you can only find one sock from a pair, the other might have become goblin food.

HABITAT

Goblins like to live in tucked-away corners where they will not be found. Their eyes are very good at seeing in the dark, so they do not need a habitat with much light.

Living outside is dangerous for goblins because there are a lot of <u>predators</u> that would happily eat them. So, they prefer to live inside human homes.

Most of the time, goblins find a dark spot inside the house of a human family. They usually settle under sinks, behind fridges, inside toilets or in basements.

Goblins hide from the humans around them. They stay hidden during the day and look for food during the night. If you hear something in the night, you might have goblins!

THE OLD GOBLIN

Goblins are said to be old once they have lived for a month. At this point in their life cycle, goblins have grown white hair. Sometimes it is on their head. Sometimes the white hair grows out of their ears and noses.

As goblins get older, the claws on their fingers grow and grow. Old goblins have very long claws.

A very old goblin can make itself young again in a truly disgusting way. When a new goblin comes from a pile of gunk, that gunk is left behind. Old goblins eat this gunk to make themselves younger.

Goblin gunk does not keep humans young. Do not eat goblin gunk!

PASSING ON
THE CURSE

The curse of the goblin is passed on by goblin spores. As well as being created by magic, goblin spores can also be made by the goblins themselves.

To make more spores, a goblin needs to eat as much as they possibly can. They stuff themselves until they are about to burst!

A drawing of a well-fed goblin.

Once the goblin is full, they get on their hands and knees. Tiny holes open all over the goblin's back. Then, they shoot a puff of spores out of these holes.

These spores get mixed into the air and end up in people's noses. When they sneeze, they let out snotty spores and the goblin's life cycle carries on.

Types of Goblin

Different kinds of gross goblins can be found in different places.

Hobgoblins

Hobgoblins are the meanest kind of goblins. They fight with each other a lot and are not afraid to be seen by humans.

Hobgoblins come from the snot of very badly behaved children. This is why it is important to behave, or else you will have nasty hobgoblins in your house!

MUCK GOBLINS

Muck goblins are the grossest kind of goblins. They are made when goblin spores get into the nose of someone with a bad cold. The snot of an unwell person makes the spores thicker and heavier.

These spores make even slimier goblin gunk. Muck goblins come out of this gunk. They are much messier than normal goblins.

SPOTTING A GOBLIN

If you think there are goblins living in your home, there are a few things that you can look for.

TISSUES

Check to see if there are any tissues wriggling around. Just because a sneeze has been caught in a tissue does not mean it has stopped goblins growing. There might be some goblins moving around inside.

BINS

Listen for squeaking around your bins. Goblins get stuck in bins when they look for food, or when tissues get used and thrown away. It might be best to tie up the bin bag and throw it out!

DIRT

Look out for tiny dirty footprints. Goblins get into all sorts of mess that sticks to the bottom of their feet.

How to Deal with a
Goblin

Nobody wants goblins in their house. Luckily, there are some ways to keep them away.

Air Fresheners

Goblins like to live in places that smell bad. Air fresheners will make the air a bit more pleasant. Nice smells chase the goblins away.

Litter

Make sure all your waste goes in the bin. Dropped rubbish could bring in hungry goblins.

CLEANING

Goblins love dirty places. Over time, parts of your house might get a bit dirty and become a hot spot for goblins.

The vacuum cleaner can suck up goblin spores that are floating around in the air.

Cleaning sprays and wet wipes can clean up sticky blobs of goblin gunk.

Wash your hands! Goblin spores can stick to dirty hands.

LIFE CYCLE OF A GOBLIN

The life cycle of a goblin starts with goblin spores. These spores get inside a person's nose and mix with their snot.

When that person sneezes, the snotty spores find a place to land. Then, goblin gunk starts to form there. Next, something starts to grow in the gunk.

Soon, a new goblin climbs out of the gunk by slashing its way out with its claws. The goblin soon becomes old, but it can stay young by finding new gunk to eat.

Goblins will shoot more spores out of their backs. These will spread in the air and later become more goblins. Then, the life cycle carries on.

BEWARE THE PARANORMAL!

There are many more paranormal creatures out in the world. You will have to be careful, though. Goblins cause a lot of trouble, but there are much more dangerous creatures creeping in the darkness.

Do not go chasing after paranormal creatures. Keep reading about them and their life cycles. Knowing about them will help you keep safe.

GLOSSARY

PESTS — creatures that damage things

PREDATORS — animals that hunt other animals for food

REPRODUCE — to make more of the same thing

SPORES — tiny things that float in the air

PARANORMAL — something that cannot be explained by science

TRANSFORM — to turn into something else

INDEX

BINS 25–26

CLAWS 12, 18, 29

GUNK 10–12, 19, 23, 27–29

NOSES 8–9, 18, 21, 23, 28

SNOT 9, 21–23, 28

SPORES 8–10, 20–21, 23, 27–29

TEETH 14

TISSUES 24–25

TOILETS 9, 17